W0010727

SWINDON
IN OLD PHOTOGRAPHS
A THIRD SELECTION

TOWN HALL AND CENOTAPH, c. 1925.

SWINDON
IN OLD PHOTOGRAPHS
A THIRD SELECTION

COLLECTED BY
THE SWINDON SOCIETY

ALAN SUTTON

Alan Sutton Publishing
Phoenix Mill · Far Thrupp · Stroud · Gloucestershire

First published 1991

Copyright © 1991 The Swindon Society

All rights reserved. No part of this publication may be reproduced, stored in a
retrieval system, or transmitted, in any form or by any means, electronic,
mechanical, photocopying, recording or otherwise, without the prior
permission of the publishers and copyright holders.

British Library Cataloguing in Publication Data

Swindon in old Photographs.
I. Swindon Society
942.313
ISBN 0-86299-907-3

The Society
wish
to dedicate this book
to Brian Bridgeman

Typeset in 9/10 Korinna.
Typesetting and origination by
Alan Sutton Publishing Limited.
Printed in Great Britain by
The Bath Press, Avon.

CONTENTS

DUKE OF EDINBURGH public house, Cricklade Road, Gorse Hill, c. 1875. Named after Prince Alfred, Duke of Edinburgh, fourth child of Queen Victoria.

SWINDON JUNCTION RAILWAY STATION FAÇADE in the 1950s.

INTRODUCTION

Although people have lived in our area for many centuries (Swindon is first mentioned by name in the Domesday survey of 1086) it took almost 1,000 years for the population of the town to rise to 1,742 in 1831, but only another 160 years to reach nearly 150,000.

We are indeed fortunate that the camera has faithfully recorded the changing face of our town over the last century or so and enabled us to have a glimpse of how our forefathers lived out their lives.

In the early 1840s, prior to the coming of the Great Western Railway, the old market town of Swindon, situated on its hill, had been bypassed by history through the years. The small parish church of Holy Rood, first mentioned in documents in 1154, stood near The Lawn, a handsome eighteenth-century mansion and home of the Goddard family, Lords of the Manor of High Swindon. The greater part of Holy Rood was demolished in 1852 after Christ Church was consecrated, and only the chancel now remains, together with the ruined pillars and arches of the former nave. This small chancel is now the only surviving building of the Swindon of the Middle Ages. For a more detailed description and history of Holy Rood see *The Story of Holy Rood: Old Parish Church of Swindon*, by Denis Bird, Swindon Society 1991.

In view of the continuing interest shown in the old parish church, the Goddard family and The Lawn, the Swindon Society has included many further views of the house and church in this volume. We also have the privilege of looking 'below stairs' at The Lawn in the 1920s, when Major Fitzroy Pleydell Goddard was Lord of the Manor.

At this time there were twelve 'indoor' staff employed: a butler, footman, cook/housekeeper, three housemaids, three kitchen maids, one between maid, one kennel maid and one 'odd job' man. Some six to eight 'outside' staff were also employed: five gardeners, two coachmen, two or three laundry maids and a keeper (who lived in a cottage in Broome Manor Lane). Electricity was not installed in The Lawn until after Major Goddard's death in 1927 and prior to this date the house was only lit by candles, except for oil lamps and one or two gas mantles in the passages. The Swindon Society is greatly indebted to the late Miss Esther Mary Elms, cook/housekeeper at The Lawn from 1918 to 1930, and Mrs Kate Cook, housemaid at The Lawn from 1918 to 1928, for much background information regarding their years 'in service' and for supplying several of the photographs reproduced here.

The everyday life of the community of Old Town continued unchanged for many years, centering on the High Street, Wood Street and Newport Street. The establishment, however, of the Great Western Railway Works in 1843 in the marshy valley some $1\frac{1}{2}$ miles to the north, instituted a long period of expansion that was to change the story of Swindon for ever. The original 'Railway Village' of some 300 terraced cottages, built to accommodate the influx of workers and their families, was neatly laid out either side of Emlyn Square (originally known as High Street, New Swindon). Soon, however, additional housing was required as the Works expanded and the local landed gentry began selling off their land to a

EMPIRE THEATRE, C. 1920. It was formerly known as the Queens Theatre but was renamed in 1906 – see *Swindon in Old Photographs (1)*. Empire House now stands on the site on the corner of Clarence Street and Groundwell Road.

GWR JUNCTION STATION, 1913. (Lens of Sutton)

growing number of hungry speculative builders. The green fields between the towns of New and Old Swindon gradually disappeared as they were swamped with terrace upon terrace of red brick houses. The railway communities of Gorse Hill and Even Swindon (Rodbourne) grew up north of the GWR Bristol–London main line during this period; even the shopping area of Bridge Street/Regent Street developed piecemeal, with shop fronts being added on to the fronts of existing terraced houses.

In 1900 the two towns became one municipal borough with a total population of 45,000.

Expansion slowed down in the first two decades of the twentieth century, but after the Second World War, when the Council decided that Swindon should become an expanding town under the Town Development Act, a second wave of building was instituted with the new estates of Penhill and Walcot. Since then expansion has continued to the present day with continuing development at West Swindon and the north. With the decline in railway engineering from the 1950s (which resulted in the final closure of the former GWR Works in 1986), new industries were attracted to the town and large industrial estates constructed. In recent years, however, many of these companies have themselves left Swindon, but the excellent communications available to London and Bristol via the M4 have attracted many new employers, both in the service and manufacturing sectors.

All these changes since the 1950s have resulted in massive and continuing redevelopment of the centre of the old railway town and, in many ways, Swindon is no longer the close-knit community it was for many years. The newcomers often know little of how the town grew up and of the lives of the old Swindonians. The Swindon Society hopes that this third collection of old photographs, together with the two preceding volumes, will stimulate newcomers to the area to learn more about Swindon and its past as well as bring back happy memories to older residents of the town.

GWR PARK, FARINGDON ROAD, c. 1905, with bandstand. In the background on the left is St Mark's church, and on the right can be seen the GWR Works Water Tower (erected in 1870).

Lords of the Manor

THE LAWN, home of the Goddard family, Lords of the Manor of Swindon. View from the south through the trees of the park, c. 1910. The house was built in about 1770, on the site of the previous medieval manor, and extended over the next 80 years. It was known as Swindon House until the early nineteenth century.

UPHAM HOUSE, C. 1910. The Goddard family of Upper Upham were major landowners in North Wiltshire and purchased the Swindon Estate in the sixteenth century. Their manor house at Upham was built upon, or near to, the site of the reputed hunting lodge of King John and John of Gaunt. It is a fine example of an Elizabethan manor house and was completed in 1599. It is now in private hands.

VIEW SOUTH TO OPEN FIELDS from the Corn Exchange Tower, 1923. To the left of the photograph can be seen the eighteenth-century Vicarage of The Planks, demolished in 1973, and centre, the stables of The Lawn (now auctioneers' salerooms). On the right is the roof of the Corn Exchange and the Wesleyan Methodist octagonal chapel. See *Swindon in Old Photographs (2)*.

VIEW EAST TO THE LAWN from the tower of the Corn Exchange, Market Square, 1923. The building to the left corner is Swindon House (see also p. 37). Excavations on the site in 1975/6 revealed Saxon remains in this area. Saxon Court and Beatty Court now stand here.

ENTRANCE GATES TO THE LAWN, High Street, after the great snowfall of April 1908.

THE LAWN, Main Entrance in High Street, c. 1930. Two single-storey lodges stood each side of the gates. These were demolished in the 1960s.

THE AVENUE, leading from High Street to The Lawn in the 1920s.

MAIN DRIVEWAY TO THE LAWN, c. 1910. To right is the Italian Garden. The bow windows belonged to the Drawing Room, which also had a large window on the north side.

MAJOR FITZROY PLEYDELL GODDARD, last Lord of the Manor of Swindon, shortly before his death in August 1927. His widow, Mrs E.K. Goddard, vacated the house in 1931. The Lawn then stood empty until the Second World War when British and American troops were billeted there, which only served to accelerate the decay.

STAFF FROM THE LAWN selling ice-cream (made from milk and cream from the estate's own Jersey cows) to raise funds for the Victoria Hospital in the 1920s.

TWO HOUSEMAIDS on the terrace of The Lawn, c. 1920.

HOUSEMAIDS AND KITCHEN MAIDS of The Lawn, 1920s. Housemaids commenced their duties at 6.30 a.m. and had one half-day off a week with, sometimes, an extra half-day on Sunday. On their half-day they had to be back on duty by 8.30 p.m. Wages were £3 to £4 a quarter, out of which they had to make or buy uniforms, morning dresses and afternoon dresses, aprons, caps and cuffs.

NORTH SIDE OF THE LAWN after the great snowfall of April 1908. This side was mainly taken up with the entrance hall.

EAST TERRACE, THE LAWN, c. 1910. On the first floor were the main bedrooms. The Dining Room was on the ground floor.

ALFRED GEORGE MILLIN, Head Coachman at The Lawn, 1907.

THE LAWN DRIVE, from Old Mill Lane, c. 1910.

GODDARD FAMILY COACH at Salisbury, 1907, when Fitzroy Pleydell Goddard was High Sherriff of Wiltshire.

THE LAWN, viewed from The Planks. To the right is the pathway to Holy Rood. The small, square windows high up on the East Wing were the staff bedrooms.

ITALIAN SUNKEN GARDEN, The Lawn, 1920s. The photograph shows the balustraded west side of the garden.

NORTH SIDE OF THE LAWN, viewed across the grounds in the 1920s. Note the early motor car in the drive. Major Goddard never learned to drive; Mrs Goddard and Miss Elms drove the car, which was owned by Mrs Goddard and kept at Skurray's Garage in High Street.

THE LAWN, from The Planks, 1930s.

THE LAWN, by now in a sad and dangerous state of dereliction, just prior to demolition in 1952.

SECTION TWO

Old Town Through the Years

HIGH STREET, looking north, C. 1918. To the left is the Bell Hotel, still with its canopy.

VICTORIA STREET, C. 1860 (now Victoria Road), looking south from a point in the centre of the road approximately level with the present entrance to Newspaper House. The buildings on the right still remain. At this time the road ended abruptly at the junction with Prospect Place.

WOOD STREET, C. 1870. This photograph was taken shortly after rebuilding of The Kings Arms Inn, seen in background.

3507   WOOD STREET.   SWINDON.

WOOD STREET, C. 1900.

WOOD STREET, looking towards the Goddard Arms, 1940s.

WOOD STREET, looking east, in the 1960s.

JUNCTION OF WOOD STREET/ALBERT STREET, 1968.

SWINDON MOTOR COMPANY, Devizes Road, 1962. This is now Fads DIY Stores.

NEWPORT STREET, looking east, c. 1900.

NEWPORT STREET, c. 1957. View west from the junction with Marlborough Road/High Street.

NEWPORT STREET/HIGH STREET JUNCTION, c. 1960. Harrisons, Newsagents, and Farrant, Wightman & Pinnegar, Estate Agents, (now Dreweatt Neate) now have premises elsewhere in Newport Street.

MASONS ARMS, High Street, c. 1950. It was demolished in 1969 for road widening, and the new Midland Bank building now stands on this site.

VIEW SOUTH DOWN HIGH STREET, to Masons Arms on right (see also p. 31), c. 1890.

HIGH STREET, looking south to the junction with Newport Street on the right, c. 1960.

CLEVERLEY'S ANTIQUE DEALERS, 34 High Street, c. 1963. To the right is the ornate doorway of Manchester House, an early eighteenth-century merchant's house. A firm of saddlers, Burge and Norris, plied their craft there for many years. All these eighteenth-century buildings are awaiting demolition for extension to Skurray's Garage, now itself demolished. The Co-op Superstore now stands on this site.

HIGH STREET, looking towards Marlborough Road, c. 1952. The splendid mock-Tudor frontage of Skurray's Garage can be seen in the background on the right.

HIGH STREET, looking north, 1950.

SNOW IN HIGH STREET, January 1962. The school sign refers to the Holy Rood Roman Catholic School, some classes of which were held at this time in huts in the grounds of The Lawn.

VIEW ACROSS THE MARKET SQUARE, looking north from the Corn Exchange Tower, 1923. The spire of Christ Church can be seen in the distance.

HIGH STREET, looking south, 1950. To the left are Lloyds Bank and Horders, ladies' outfitters.

DR BEATTY'S HOUSE AND GARDEN, 1927. Looking west toward Corn Exchange tower. A glimpse of Skurray's Garage in High Street in the process of being rebuilt can just be seen next to the tower.

SWINDON HOUSE, Market Square, Old Town, c. 1930. The house at this time was the home of Dr Beatty. Now sheltered flats stand on this site. Dr Beatty's watch is displayed there.

DR R.P. BEATTY, surgeon, relaxing in his garden with his small daughter, 1927.

COACH OUTSIDE THE GODDARD ARMS, High Street, 1900. An inn has stood on this site for 400 years. Formerly known as The Crown, it was rebuilt and renamed around the end of the eighteenth century and was used to house the local Magistrates Court for several years.

E. SMITH'S BUTCHER'S SHOP, High Street, c. 1910. The building was formerly The King of Prussia Inn, a public house of ill repute. The premises remained a family butcher's shop until demolition in 1981. A superficially similar office building, Eastcott House, has now been built on the site.

COPSON'S TOY SHOP, 11 Bath Road, 1968. Now Hats – The Finishing Touch.

VICTORIA ROAD, looking south, c. 1950. To the left is the post office and the site of the Congregational church (see p. 107).

'THE CHOC SHOP', 97 Victoria Road, 1968.

BATH ROAD, looking west, C. 1910. To the right is the Wesleyan Methodist church (opened in 1880).

FIRST MEET OF THE SEASON, Kingshill House, C. 1910. The Vale of White Horse Hunt met in various places in Old Town including the Market Square, High Street. In 1931 this large house was acquired, extended and opened as a maternity hospital by Swindon Corporation. Today it is the Seymour Clinic.

GODDARD AVENUE, c. 1910.

VICTORIA HOSPITAL, Okus Road, Christmas celebrations, c. 1910. The hospital opened in September 1888, with accommodation for twelve patients. Various enlargements and extensions took place over the years but it finally closed in 1991.

THE MALL, 1913. These stylish Edwardian houses were only about five years old at this time.

OKUS ROAD, looking west, 1922.

LOWER TOWN (MARLBOROUGH ROAD), looking north, c. 1950. On the left can be seen various small shops and cottages leading to the junction with Newport Street.

ARCADING on the rear wall of an outbuilding of the Bell and Shoulder of Mutton public house, 1960s. This was the only remains of the former Wesleyan Methodist chapel, The Planks, demolished in 1937.

MARLBOROUGH ROAD, looking north to High Street, April 1960.

ENTRANCE ROAD TO SWINDON TOWN GOODS DEPOT (Midland & South Western Junction Railway), Coate Road, c. 1910, with horse-drawn wagons. This is now Signal Way, Marlborough Road.

COATE ROAD, junction with Broome Manor Lane to the right, in the 1920s.

BROOME MANOR LANE, looking north. The photograph was taken during the winter of 1946/7.

New Swindon: Streets, Shops, Trade and Industry

CROMWELL STREET, looking towards Regent Street, c. 1910. To the right is W.H. Hooper, photographer, whom we have to thank for many of the best and most evocative views of Swindon at this period.

F.W. WILLIAMS, FISH RESTAURANT, 2 Market Street, c. 1920.

THE WILLIAMS FAMILY (with fish) outside the rear of their shop in the 1920s.

THE MARKET, viewed from Cromwell Street, c. 1960. Opened in 1892, it was closed in 1977 and demolished. The area is used as car park today, but there are plans to build another market on the same site.

CURTIS STREET, viewed from the Market, 1913. On the right on the corner of Milton Road is Franklins, decorators' merchants, later in Cromwell Street and Stratton Road.

BRIDGE STREET, looking south from Tram Centre, 1906. (Lens of Sutton)

VIEW SOUTH UP BRIDGE STREET, from junction with Fleet Street, 1957.

BRIDGE STREET, looking north, c. 1906. (Lens of Sutton)

INTERIOR OF BOOTS THE CHEMISTS, 27/28 Bridge Street, c. 1910. Peacocks now have a shop on this site.

KNOX & SADDLER, DRAPERS, 50–54 Bridge Street, c. 1910. Comet now stands on this site.

WEAVER TO WEARER LTD, 'The 30/– Tailors', 44 Bridge Street, 1945. Keogh Bros, next door, still retained its Victorian façade at this time and remained in business until the mid-1960s.

KEOGH BROS, HARDWARE STORE, 45 Bridge Street, during their opening sale in 1901. Superdrug stood on the site until recently.

JOHN DREW, PRINTER AND STATIONER, 51 Bridge Street, c. 1910.

BRIDGE STREET, view north, 1913. On the right is The Rolling Mills public house (now Porter's Café Bar) on the corner of King Street.

MONTAGUE BURTON, TAILORS, 92 Regent Street, 1945.

REGENT STREET, looking south, c. 1925. To the right is the Fox Tavern (on the corner of Cromwell Street), and on the left is the Eagle Hotel (on the corner of College Street).

W. VEAL, JEWELLERS, 87 Regent Street, c. 1910. Marks and Spencers now occupy this site.

REGENT STREET, looking north, c. 1910. On the right is the recently opened County Electric Pavilion, Swindon's first cinema. Woolworth's store now stands on this site.

J.H. JONES, UMBRELLA MANUFACTURERS, 57 Regent Street, c. 1910. Today Foto Processing stands on this site.

WILLIAM McILROY'S DEPARTMENT STORE, with original clock tower, 1945. The tower was built by John Norman, an Old Town builder who had his office in Victoria Road. This imposing landmark was demolished during the refurbishment of the store in the mid-1960s.

REGENT STREET, looking north, c. 1963. To the left is John Anstiss department store, on the corner of Havelock Street, shortly to suffer the serious fire which destroyed it. On the right is the Classic Cinema.

REGENT STREET, looking north, with the junction with Edgeware Road to the right, 1960s.

HAVELOCK STREET, looking towards Regent Street, 1968.

REGENT STREET, looking south, 1950s.

JAMES WALKER, JEWELLERS, 26 Regent Street, 1945. James Walker traded here for many years, but the shop is now Zales jewellers.

ENTRANCE TO JAMES WALKER, Regent Street, 1945.

ARTHUR DAY, 'Where Mother buys fruit, flowers and coal', 63 Regent Street, 1945. Note how many generations of customers have worn down the front step. The shop is now Pizzaland.

INTERIOR OF DAY'S, 1945.

CELLARS UNDER DAY'S SHOP, 1945, where flowers were kept cool.

INTERIOR OF 'THE SPOT', 60 Regent Street, 1945, where many Swindonians used to buy their cycles, sports equipment and models. Now Swiss Chalet, Bakers, is on this site.

J. LOTT & SONS, IRONMONGERS, 50–51 Regent Street, c. 1910. J. Lott & Sons traded also as Plumbers and Heating Engineers at these premises until the 1960s. Now Burger King stands on this site.

REGENT STREET, looking south, c. 1956. On the right can be seen the Primitive Methodist church and H. Howell, Chemists. These and other buildings were shortly to be demolished in the first redevelopment of the town centre.

REGENT STREET, looking north, from near Regent Circus, 1928. Note the Central Hotel, on the site of the Savoy/ABC/Cannon Cinema to the right. To the left is the Primitive Methodist church.

REGENT STREET, looking north from near Savoy Cinema (opened 1937), c. 1939. The cinema closed in 1991.

TOWN HALL, prior to the building of the 'temporary' library at the rear, c. 1950.

REGENT CIRCUS, with the corner of Rolleston Street on the left and the Bristol Omnibus Company office, August 1967.

REGENT CIRCUS, looking towards Commercial Road, 1960s.

PRINCES STREET, with Constitutional Conservative Club to the left, December 1964.

PRINCES STREET, between Regent Circus and Regents Place, October 1964.

REGENTS PLACE, from Princes Street, September 1960. To the right is the junction with Cow Lane, one of the original roads of Swindon that pre-dated the coming of the railway.

CORNER OF PRINCES STREET AND GORDON ROAD, looking south with the area under redevelopment, October, 1964.

CHELTENHAM STREET, looking north, February 1970. Beales Snack Bar is on the left at the junction with Fleet Street. This area is now covered with new office blocks, but a small section of roadway has been named Beales Close.

G.A. BRISTOW, GENERAL STORES, 35 Manchester Road (corner of Gladstone Street), 1925.

F.H. SEXTONE'S MILK CART, C. 1912. Their dairy was at 32 Manchester Road. Fred Sextone is pictured here with 'Little Jolly' the pony. Their advertising slogans were: 'Families waited on twice daily'; 'Fresh butter, Pure new milk'; 'Special milk for infants'; 'A trade respectfully solicited'.

COUNTY ROAD, looking north, C. 1905. No houses had been built at that time on the west side of the road.

SARAH J. HEARLE, DRAPERS & MILLINERS, 40–41 Cricklade Road, c. 1905. Now various small shops including the Sue Ryder Gift Shop stand on this site.

REDCLIFFE STREET, c. 1905.

L. GRIFFIN, FISH FRYER, Groves Street, Rodbourne, c. 1920.

ELECTRICITY WORKS, Corporation Street, *c.* 1910. The Works opened in 1903 on the site formerly occupied by Lower Eastcott Farm – see *Swindon in Old Photographs (1)*. The chimney was 150 ft high.

TYDEMAN'S BUILDERS, 1 Edgeware Road, 1930s. Note the different spellings of Sanford Street; this is also apparent on the school at the other end of the street.

QUEEN STREET WORKS of New Swindon Gas Company, c. 1870. Built 1863/4. Murray John Tower now stands on this site.

QUEEN STREET GAS WORKS, cooker repair shop, 1919. Left to right: Fred Haydon, Norman Speck, Bill Kilford, Ted Butcher and George Uzzell.

THE PARADE, west side, looking east, January 1970. The rear of Crornwell Street can be seen to the right. To the left is the Co-operative Society furniture store.

CO-OPERATIVE SOCIETY 'ECONOMY' FURNITURE STORE, The Parade, January 1970. Formerly part of Queen Street gasworks.

SECTION FOUR

Canals, Trams and Road Transport

VIEW WEST TO GOLDEN LION BRIDGE along the Wilts & Berks Canal (the junction of the North Wilts Canal is to the right), 1914. On the left is College Street School, with the playground directly overlooking the canal. The pedestrian footbridge (see overleaf) at the Golden Lion Bridge had been removed by this date. By this time the canal was in a sorry state, and it was abandoned under an Act of 1914.

GOLDEN LION CANAL BRIDGE, c. 1908, showing details of raised pedestrian overbridge. In the background is the Wilts and Somerset Bank in Regent Street.

GOLDEN LION BRIDGE, looking east from canal towpath, c. 1908.

GOLDEN LION BRIDGE, Wilts & Berks Canal, c. 1908. A favourite scene of old Swindon used as the basis for a mural near Whale Bridge Roundabout. This iron lift bridge, at the junction of Regent Street and Bridge Street, took its name from the adjacent Golden Lion public house. It was built in the GWR Works and replaced the original wooden swing bridge in 1870. The fixed pedestrian footbridge was added by public subscription in 1877 – previously men at the GWR Works were often late for work when the bridge was up. The bridge was demolished in 1918 – see *Swindon in Old Photographs (1)*.

GENTS IRON URINAL, near Golden Lion Bridge, 1908, with contemporary advertising posters on the wall.

FLEET STREET BRIDGE, over North Wilts Canal, looking north from John Street bridge, 1914.

CROMWELL STREET WHARF, Wilts & Berks Canal, 1896. The canal had been blocked to lay the foundations of the new Central Club and Institute – see *Swindon in Old Photographs (2)*. In the distance to the left is the Golden Lion Bridge.

WILTS & BERKS CANAL, looking east, near Marlborough Street/Read Street, 1914.

KINGSHILL BRIDGE, over Wilts & Berks Canal, looking south-west, September 1910. The bridge was constructed in 1803 and demolished in the 1920s.

TELFORD ROAD (NOW RODBOURNE ROAD) BRIDGE, over North Wilts Canal, viewed from the west, 1912. Constructed around 1815, the bridge was demolished in the early 1920s. It was situated where the footpath from Iffley Road meets Rodbourne Road, next to the petrol station.

DRIED UP BED of North Wilts Canal, view west from Telford Road Bridge, 1912.

WHALE BRIDGE, over dried up bed of Wilts & Berks Canal, looking east, in 1960. To the left is the Victorian men's urinal and, in the background, H.C. Preater's garage, now Walker Jackson's. (See also p. 93.)

SITE OF DROVE ROAD CANAL BRIDGE, Wilts & Berks Canal, looking east, 1955.

TRAMCAR AT GWR PARK, 1906. The tramway system opened in September 1904. Its focal point was the Fleet Street / Bridge Street junction, known from then on as The Centre. From here routes went to Gorse Hill, Rodbourne and the Market Square, Old Town, with a short branch also to the GWR Junction Station. The tramcar shown above was one of those purchased from Dick Kerr & Co., Preston, and had been brought to the Midland & South Western Junction Railway Station in Old Town by rail. Livery was cream and crimson lake. It was fitted with a Tidswell lifeguard, a device which automatically dropped to road level on encountering an obstacle, preventing any person passing under the wheels. Gauge of permanent way was 3 ft 6 in.

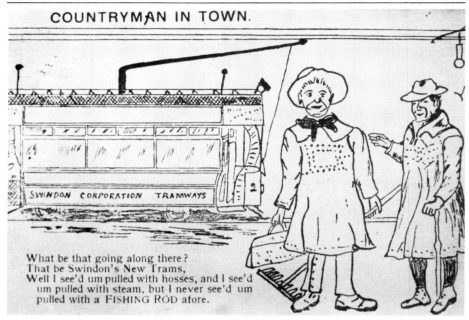

CARTOON issued at the time of the coming of tramways to Swindon, 1904.

FLEET STREET JUNCTION WITH BRIDGE STREET, looking east, c. 1905.

PARK LANE, looking north to Rodbourne Lane, in the summer of 1910. To right is GWR Park, site of the Mechanics Institute children's fête.

TRAMCAR IN PARK LANE, looking north, c. 1910. (Lens of Sutton)

DECORATED TRAMCAR, Coronation of King George V and Queen Mary, June 1911. There were two hundred coloured lights on the vehicle.

FARINGDON ROAD, looking east, c. 1906. In the background is the Wesleyan Methodist chapel (now the Railway Museum). (Lens of Sutton)

FLEET STREET, looking east, 1910. On the left is the Sir Daniel Arms public house.

SWINDON CORPORATION TRAMWAY STAFF at Swindon Town (MSWJR) Station, c. 1919, wishing 'bon voyage' to conductor Jack Lewis who was emigrating to Canada. Left to right: -?-, G. Nicholls and E. Strudwick (conductors), postman Glass (ex-conductor), W. Stroud and H. Hulbert (drivers), H. Hobbs (conductor), ex-conductor J. Lewis (in train), Driver Lewis, Inspector J. Minto, Driver G. Ellery, J. Chislett and F. Neate (conductors), Inspector F. Wiltshire.

FLEET STREET, looking east from near Bridge Street, c. 1912. To the right is the Oxford Hotel, where Beatties toy and sports shop now stands.

BRIDGE STREET, looking north, c. 1906. (Lens of Sutton)

CONDUCTOR W. REEVES (in train) leaves Corporation Tramways for a new life in Australia, Swindon GWR Station, c. 1920. Staff, left to right: Inspector F. Wiltshire, Drivers C. Lammas and Reeves, Conductor Cathcart, Driver J. Cairns, Conductors C. Simpson and Wright, Driver Reeves sen., W. Pagington (conductor), Driver Pearce, D. Constable (conductor), Inspector J. Minto, F. Cole and F. Avenell (conductors), H. Hulbert (driver), E. Strudwick and J. Chislett (conductors), G. Ellery (driver).

THE LAST TRAM at Bruce Street Terminus, 11 July 1929. Although of poor quality, this photograph is of historic importance. Tramcar No. 1, gaily decorated and driven by motorman George Cathcart, made its last journey over the Gorse Hill to Rodbourne route.

THE FIRST BUS at Bruce Street Terminus, July 1929. Fifteen Leyland Titan open-rear staircase vehicles were purchased to replace the trams.

DR BEATTY'S CAR, 1930s. (See also p. 37.)

H.C. PREATER'S GARAGE, Princes Street, looking north to Whale Bridge, 1920s.

MORRIS STREET CLUB OUTING, visiting Gough's Cave, Cheddar, c. 1913.

RIMES CENTRAL GARAGE, with Princes Street to the rear, 1920s. Originally this was the site of the Swindon Charabanc Company.

RIMES COACHES, BOOKING OFFICE, Princes Street, c. 1969. They were about to move to Commercial Road, where they survived until the early 1980s.

ARKELL'S BREWERY STAFF on an outing to Southsea in the 1920s.

WOOTTON BASSETT ROAD after floods in the 1930s. It was said that Farmer Ball of Toothill towed out stranded cars with his horse and cart from the floods at 2s. 6d. (12½p) a time.

Churches, Chapels and Schools

CHILDREN IN HOLY ROOD CHURCHYARD, The Planks, 1896.

VIEW FROM JUNCTION OF THE PLANKS and Old Mill Lane in 1847. The drawing is by John Luckett Jefferies, a relative of the writer Richard Jefferies. In the background is Holy Rood, then complete with its tower – see photograph in *Swindon in Old Photographs (1)*. In the foreground stands the mill, which was driven by water from the church pond. The mill survived until the 1850s.

CHANCEL OF HOLY ROOD, viewed from churchyard, after the snowfall of April 1908.

VICTORIAN CHILDREN in front of the ivy covered chancel of Holy Rood, 1896.

BAPTIST CHAPEL, FLEET STREET, C. 1880. The first general Baptist chapel in Swindon, it was opened in 1849. The congregation moved to the Baptist Tabernacle, Regent Circus, in 1886, after which the Fleet Street chapel was demolished. Some remains can still be seen behind the music shop there now.

FLEET STREET, looking towards Faringdon Road from junction with Bridge Street, C. 1880. On the right is the Baptist church, and in the distance can be seen the Wesleyan Methodist chapel.

REGENT CIRCUS, 1950, looking towards the rear of the Methodist Central Hall.

BAPTIST TABERNACLE, Regent Circus, 1973. This impressive building, with its massive portico of columns, was built in 1886. It was demolished in 1978, and The Pilgrim Centre, opened in November 1990, now occupies the site.

PRIMITIVE METHODIST CHURCH, Regent Street, c. 1956. Pearl Assurance House now stands on this site.

WELLINGTON STREET, looking south, 1967. The Hambro building (now Allied Dunbar) is under construction. To the right is the Railway Mission, where many generations of Swindon railwaymen worshipped. It was destroyed by fire in 1979.

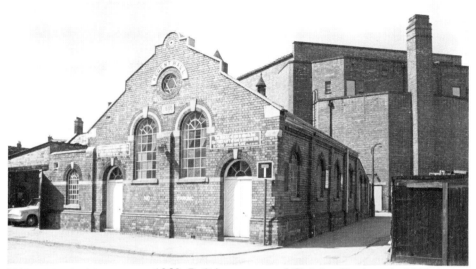

REGENTS PLACE GOSPEL HALL, 1968. Built by a group of Christian Brethren in 1899, it was demolished around 1970 for the redevelopment of the Princes Street area. In the background is the rear of the Savoy/ABC Cinema.

TRINITY PRESBYTERIAN CHURCH and 'Radio Relay', Victoria Road, 1954. The church on the junction with Groundwell Road was built in 1899 and used until the congregation moved to the new Pilgrim Centre in Regent Circus in 1990.

REHOBOTH PARTICULAR BAPTIST CHAPEL, Prospect Hill, 1968. First registered as a meeting-place for Particular Baptists in 1882.

CHRIST CHURCH, viewed from Church Road, 1930s.

VICTORIA ROAD, viewed from junction with Bath Road, c. 1930. This view shows how narrow the street was at this time – to the left stands the Congregational church and the original shops.

THE BIBLE INSTITUTE, Devizes Road, c. 1925. Licensed as an Evangelical church and Bible Institute in 1923.

CONGREGATIONAL CHURCH, junction of Victoria Road and Bath Road, c. 1905. Built in 1886, it was demolished in 1949.

CAMBRIA PLACE BAPTIST CHAPEL, 1968. Built in 1866 for the Welshmen and their families who came to Swindon around this time to work in the GWR Works. For many years the sermons were preached in Welsh. It finally closed in 1986.

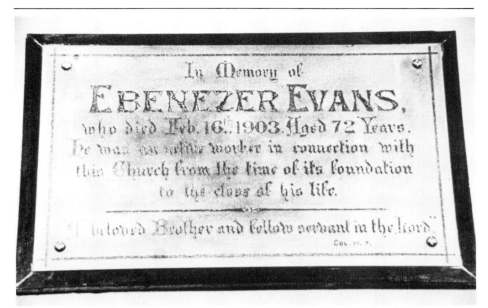

PLAQUE TO EBENEZER EVANS in Cambria Place Chapel.

CAMBRIA BAPTIST CHAPEL CHRISTIAN ENDEAVOUR TREAT, c. 1930. The outing consisted of a trip through Shaw, then round the Lydiards to picnic at Mr William Ball's farm at Toothill.

CAMBRIA CHAPEL SUNDAY SCHOOL TREAT, Marlborough Forest, 18 August 1928.

CAMBRIA BAPTIST CHAPEL SUNDAY SCHOOL TREAT, 18 August 1928, to Marlborough Forest. Back row, left to right: Mr Fred Clarke, Mrs Clarke, Miss A. Mills, -?-, Mrs Sissy Smith, Charles Hurley, Mr Charles Smith, Cyril Davis. Second row: Miss Jones, Maud Howell, Ella Clark, Miss Tucker. Front row: -?-.

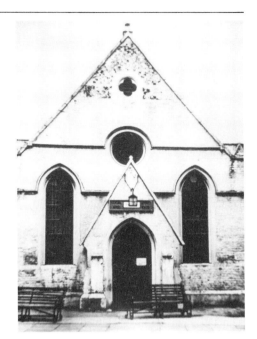

(OLD) BAPTIST CHURCH, Gorse Hill, c. 1960. Built near the corner of Cricklade Road and Ferndale Road around 1883, it was used as such until 1904. The building was not, however, demolished and was used, at this time, as the Plessey Club. A new façade was later built across the old frontage.

RODBOURNE ROAD BAPTIST MISSION CHAPEL, c. 1960. This iron church and schoolroom, formerly used by troops on Salisbury Plain, was erected in 1907. It closed in 1964. Sheltered flats now stand on the site.

VIEW NORTH TO ST MARY'S CHURCH, Rodbourne Cheney, 1930s.

ST MARY'S CHURCH BAND OF HOPE, Rodbourne Cheney, c. 1910. The photograph was taken outside the old vicarage.

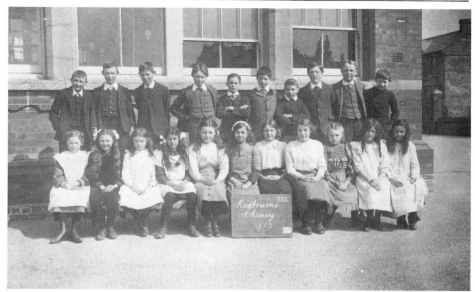

RODBOURNE CHENEY SCHOOL GROUP, 1915.

KING WILLIAM STREET SCHOOL, classroom and pupils, c. 1920.

FERNDALE ROAD SCHOOL, 1917. Now used as the Adult Education Section of North Star College.

GROUP AT PINEHURST INFANTS' SCHOOL. The school was opened in 1930 using temporary accommodation.

EUCLID STREET SCHOOL 1ST XI FOOTBALL TEAM, 1930s. The photograph was taken outside the front of the school. Mr D. McLean is the teacher on the left of the photograph.

SWINDON AND NORTH WILTSHIRE TECHNICAL INSTITUTE, Victoria Road, c. 1910. Opened in 1896, it was reorganized as a college of further education in 1926 and renamed The College the following year.

CLASS IN GORSE HILL SCHOOL, Avening Street, 1920s.

CLASS IN LETHBRIDGE ROAD SCHOOL, 1930s.

Swindonians Through the Years: Work, Life and Leisure

RUSTIC BRIDGE, Town Gardens, c. 1910. The view was wrongly captioned by Messrs Tomkins & Barrett, who issued this postcard view.

GWR WORKS DRAWING OFFICE. The staff are shown during their last day in old cramped accommodation before moving to a new office in 1924.

GWR LOCO DEPARTMENT, Swindon Break-down Gang, January 1936.

VIEW SOUTH from the rear garden of a house in Ferndale Road, c. 1926, before Harcourt Road was built. In the background is the vertical retort house of the railway gasworks, completed in 1922.

FAMILY GROUP in the rear garden of a house in Cricklade Road, 1920s.

TYPICAL GARDEN of a terraced house, St Margaret's Road, Old Town, 1903.

Swindon Boro' Military Prize Band.

Winners of National Military Band Championship,
Crystal Palace, Sept. 25th, 1909.

Conductor :—
F. G. DAVIS,
16, Volta Road,

Hon. Secretary :—
Mr. A. G. THEOBALD,
1, Horsell Street
Swind

SWINDON BOROUGH MILITARY BAND, winners of the Brass Band Championship at Crystal Palace, September 1909.

SWINDON CYCLE CLUB at Lechlade, 1919. Note Inglesham Round House, on the Thames and Severn Canal, in the background.

SWINDON WHEELERS BICYCLE CLUB, 1920. Left to right: Ernest Cater, William McLeod, Maria Cater, Meterice Simpson.

EVEN SWINDON UNITED FC, 1913/14.

POWDER WORKS LADIES FOOTBALL TEAM, 1917. A vast munitions works was established off Gipsy Lane to produce ammonia nitrite in 1916. An army of young women were employed here in the First World War, working a twelve hour shift, seven days a week, for a wage of 30s. (£1.50) a week, which was considered very good at the time.

REFUGEES FROM HOLLAND. Pierse and Henrietta Stas with Nellie Beasley, daughter of Mr and Mrs J.B. Beesley, Wholesale Fruiterer, with whom they were billeted in Curtis Street during the First World War.

WEDDING GROUP in garden of a house in Redcliffe Street, Rodbourne, c. 1916. Note the bridegroom and a guest in army uniform.

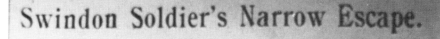

Swindon Soldier's Narrow Escape.

SERGEANT ARTHUR LOVEDAY, of the 1st Wilts Regt., son of Mr. Paul Loveday, 106 Stafford Street, Swindon, has experienced some narrow escapes in the great war. He is 28 years of age, an ex-soldier, and was a Private when he went to France on the outbreak of hostilities. He was quickly promoted to Corporal, and then to Sergeant.

Sergeant Loveday had previously spent a year in India with his Regiment, and was in the Reserve when called up. He was in the battle of Mons, where he was wounded in the thigh, being sent home to recover, and was wounded a second time in the face, for which he was treated in Hospital. For some time he acted as a guard on the lines of communication, ultimately rejoining his Regiment. At Hooge he had a very narrow escape. He received a shot in his bandolier, being fired at by a German sniper as he was making his way to the trenches. The bullet penetrated and became securely embedded in two cartridges, denting a third and the clip in which they were contained. Luckily the cartridges did not explode.

The photograph above shows the cartridges pierced by the German bullet.

SERGEANT LOVEDAY'S BULLET — a postcard from the First World War.

WEST SWINDON WORKMEN'S CLUB FOOTBALL CLUB, 1922/3. Back row, left to right: H. Gardiner (Committee), J. Skinner, W. Hooper, F. Tyler, F. Turk (Vice-President). Second row: W. Lowe (Trainer), E. Goldsmith (Committee), W. Oakley, J.C. McLeod, W. Mayell, G. Tyler (Committee), H. Price (Asst Hon Sec). Front row: W. Kirk (Hon Sec), F.L. Hathaway, W. McLeod (Chairman), W. Newman (Captain), J. Tyler. In front: A. Clack.

WEST SWINDON CLUB, **48/49** Radnor Street, c. 1920. In the early hours of Thursday 4 October 1923 the premises were devastated by a serious fire which caused much damage to the building and contents.

CHOIRBOYS OF ST AUGUSTINE'S CHURCH, with Canon Harvey, at Sunday School Treat, c. 1920s, on Jones's field, where Fosse and Watling Close now stand.

SCHOOL SPORTS DAY, County Ground Extension, 1920s.

EDWARDS' FAMILY BAND. Prior to the age of radio, television and the leisure industry explosion, families made their own entertainment. This photograph was taken in Thomas Street in the 1920s.

CELLULAR CLOTHING COMPANY LTD, Morris Street. This photograph was taken at the opening of the Sports Ground at the rear of the factory in Rose Street, 1938. The property was taken over by Morses in the 1950s and the sports ground area developed as a warehouse extension. This later became Kay's mail order warehouse. Demolished in the 1980s, it is now a residential area of houses and flats.

CIVIL DEFENCE CASUALTY SERVICE, Broad Street Ambulance Dept HQ, St Luke's Church Hall, 1941.

ST BARNABAS' SCOUTS (formed in 1932), c. 1944.

High Days and Holidays

QUEEN VICTORIA'S DIAMOND JUBILEE, 1897. Crowds gathered under a decorated arch in County Road to the south side of Gorse Hill railway bridge. This is the view towards Manchester Road. See also *Swindon in Old Photographs (1)*.

CELLULAR CLOTHING COMPANY (Shirt Factory), Morris Street. The factory opened in 1902, and this photograph shows a bazaar in the factory in 1910.

VIEW OF STALLS in the bazaar at Cellular Clothing Factory, 1910.

WOOD STREET, decorated to celebrate the Golden Jubilee of Queen Victoria in June 1887.

REGENT CIRCUS. Baptist Tabernacle and Regent Street from Town Hall, August 1902.

SHOPS IN REGENT CIRCUS, 1902. Regent Street has been decorated for the Coronation of King Edward VII.

BELL HOTEL, HIGH STREET, decorated to celebrate the Coronation of King Edward VII in August 1902. An inscription over the entrance claims it was established in 1515, although the present building dates from the early nineteenth century when it was a major coaching inn and departure point for the tri-weekly London coach. It was also the post office for Swindon in the 1830s.

TOWN HALL decorated for the Coronation of King George V, June 1911.

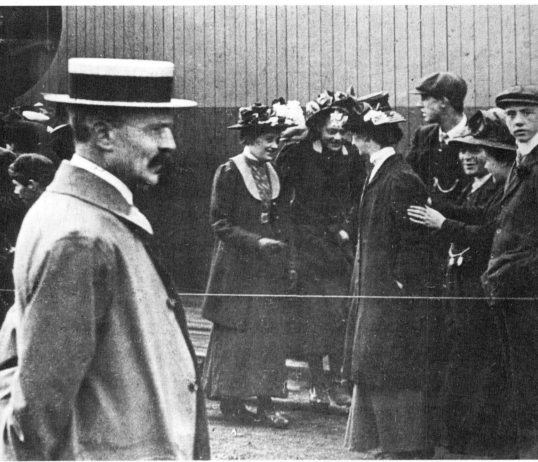

'TRIP', C. 1910. This was the annual holiday for Railway Swindon. An eagle-eyed supervisor ensures that the excited families of Swindon railwaymen do not trespass beyond the barriers, while waiting for their trains in the Works sidings.

GWR MECHANICS INSTITUTE CHILDRENS FÊTE, c. 1910. Held in The Park on the second Saturday in August, this was the great social event of the year in Swindon from 1868 to 1939.

GWR CHILDREN'S FÊTE, c. 1910. Another view.

GWR PARK, Gardens, c. 1893.

SWINDON CONSERVATIVE AND UNIONIST ASSOCIATION CHARABANC OUTING, 1920s. The photograph was taken outside the Association Rooms at 17 Regent Circus.

NORTH SWINDON CLUB OUTING on River Thames, c. 1924.

SWINDON CARNIVAL PRINCESS and attendants, 1930s.

QUEEN MARY in the GWR Works, during the royal visit of 28 April 1924. A lady wearing her best overall is making luggage rack netting.

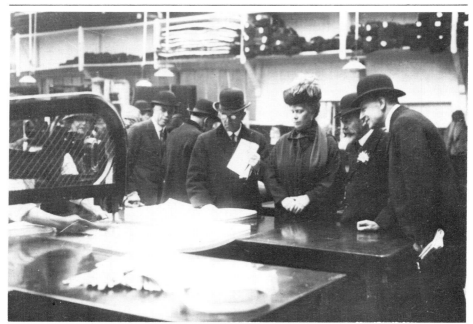

QUEEN MARY in the GWR Works, during her visit to the Carriage Works (trimming department).

KING GEORGE V, royal visit in April 1924, during a tour of the wheel turning and balancing section of the A W Shop.

KING GEORGE V, royal visit to GWR Works, 28 April 1924, watching a railwayman turning a 100-ton locomotive on the 65 ft turntable.

EXMOUTH STREET PARTY, to celebrate the Silver Jubilee of King George V and Queen Mary, 1935. The photograph was taken in Clifton Street Infants' School yard.

VE DAY STREET PARTY, May 1945, in Shipton Grove, Old Walcot.

REGENT CIRCUS DECORATIONS for the Coronation of Queen Elizabeth II, June 1953.

CORONATION STREET PARTY in Bright Street, Gorse Hill, June 1953.

GORSE HILL SCHOOL CORONATION CELEBRATIONS, June 1953.

CORONATION CELEBRATIONS in Bright Street, Gorse Hill, June 1953.

SECTION EIGHT

Some
Outlying Villages

NANNY, MISS PAGE, Wroughton, c. 1900. The location is possibly Perry's Lane.

WROUGHTON WORKHOUSE COTTAGES, c. 1890. These were situated at the lower end of Markham Road (also known as Workhouse Road).

AFTERMATH OF GREAT FIRE OF WROUGHTON, July 1896. This started in the rick yard of King's Farm, and due to the hot, dry weather quickly spread to the thatched cottages on both sides of the High Street. Over one hundred people were rendered homeless.

WROUGHTON, looking west from near Ely Inn (now The Wroughton) along High Street, c. 1905.

DEVIZES ROAD, WROUGHTON, c. 1905. A family group in front of their thatched cottage – A.K. Woodworking Ltd now occupy this site.

WROUGHTON, c. 1910. Sam Pickett and family in front of their cottage behind the Church Institute in the High Street.

WHARF ROAD, WROUGHTON, with Ellendune Hall to the right, c. 1900. The latter was demolished in the 1970s for the new Ellendune shopping centre, but the section of iron railing remains to this day.

ENTRANCE TO ELLENDUNE HALL, Wharf Road, Wroughton, c. 1920. Notice the new Daimler motor car.

WROUGHTON JUNIOR TEMPERANCE FOOTBALL TEAM, Artis Farm, North Wroughton, C. 1905. Provisional identifications are, left to right: Billy James, Ernest Middleton, George Ovens, George Jefferies, -?-, Willy Weston, Bill Baker, Charlie Stone, Charlie Cowley, Percy Hinder, Ernest Jefferies, Arthur Griffin.

BURDEROP PARK MANOR HOUSE, C. 1910. A Georgian manor set in extensive grounds, this was the property of the Calley family from the seventeenth century. Today it is a business centre, the premises of Sir William Halcrow & Partners Ltd, Consulting Engineers.

PLOUGH INN, Badbury, 1953.

POST OFFICE AND PRIMITIVE METHODIST CHURCH, Ermin Street, Stratton St Margaret, c. 1905. The post office moved to its present location, near the Crown Inn, shortly after the First World War.

THE POST OFFICE AND CROWN INN (to the left), Ermin Street, Stratton St Margaret, c. 1920.

ERMIN STREET, Stratton St Margaret, looking north c. 1910. To the left is the old vicarage.

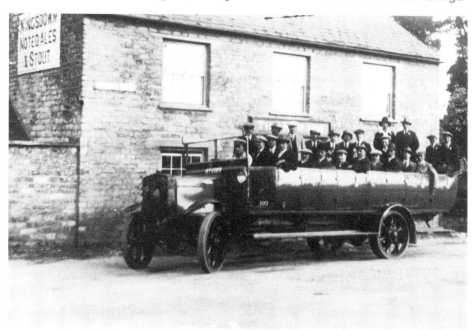

OUTING FROM NEW INN, Stratton St Margaret, with Bristol Tramways & Carriage Co. charabanc, 1920s.

PHILLIPS AND POWIS AIRCRAFT FACTORY, South Marston, 1941. An aerial view looking south – Highworth Road is to the right. A 'shadow factory' for large scale production of training aircraft was built at South Marston in 1940, many Miles Master II & III versions being assembled there for the Royal Air Force. The bombing of Short's aircraft factory at Rochester in 1940 resulted in that company establishing a major Stirling heavy bomber production line there. Nearby, at Stratton St Margaret, they also set up drawing office facilities. The company used the factory and adjacent airfield until the end of the Second World War.

From 1943, Vickers Armstrongs Ltd established a satellite production unit for Spitfire fighter aircraft at South Marston, and this continued after the end of the Second World War. Some of the last marks of Spitfire and Seafire (the naval version of the Spitfire) were built there.

Aircraft production continued after the war and many prototype and service aircraft were produced over these years: the Spiteful and Seafang (developments from the Spitfire); the first Royal Navy jet fighter, the Attacker; the Swift fighter (which held the world air speed record for a time in the 1950s) and the Scimitar naval fighter. Today most of the old factory buildings have been demolished and Honda are erecting their new car production facility on the airfield.

MAP (MINISTRY OF AIRCRAFT PRODUCTION) BUNGALOWS at Kingsdown, Upper Stratton, 1953. These, with others at Moredon, were hastily built during the Second World War, mainly to house workers at Short Brothers at South Marston, Blunsdon St Andrew and Sevenhampton, when the factory moved up from Rochester to escape the bombing.

ST PHILLIP'S ROAD, Upper Stratton, near the junction with Beechcroft Road, 1920s.

STATION ROAD, Stratton St Margaret, c. 1910. The rise in the distant road is the bridge over the Highworth branch line at Stratton Station.

STANTON STATION, on Highworth branch railway, c. 1918. On the right is Mr T. Shergold, station master from 1918 to 1925.

PURTON SPA, PURTON STOKE, *c.* 1893. It was developed by a Dr Samuel Sadler of Purton Court in 1860 and the spa water was sold at Swindon market, in the Market Square off High Street, for some years. Later a Mr Neville took water around Swindon and district by pony and trap and then by car until 1940, selling it at 8d. a bottle or 1s. carriage paid.

ACKNOWLEDGEMENTS

The Swindon Society would like to thank all members and friends who helped to compile this third volume of old photographs of Swindon. Especial thanks are due to Jean Allen and Brian Bridgeman who undertook the task of selecting the photographs to be used from the wealth of material available. Also Society members Denis Bird, Bill Brettell, Richard and Lydia Clarke, Tony Daglish, Colin Herbert and Colin McLeod for providing photographs from their collections and Denis, once again, for several taken with his own perceptive camera around Swindon in the 1960s. The Society would also like to express its gratitude to all other members and friends who supplied photographs and information. Unfortunately, again, not all photographs supplied could be used due to limitations on the space available.

Our thanks also go to Mr Roger Trayhurn and the staff of Swindon Reference Library (Wiltshire Library and Museum Service), Borough of Thamesdown Museums Service, Mr David Marchant of Ridgeway Studios, the *Evening Advertiser*, J. Arkell & Sons Ltd, Lens of Sutton, Vickers plc. and Mr Tom Cliffe. Also former Swindon Society secretary, David Luker, who originally obtained many of the photographs in the Society Collection. For individual contributions the Swindon Society would also like to thank:

Mrs J. Allen, • Mr D. Barrett • Mr B. Bridgeman

Mr R. Burbidge • Mrs K. Cook • Mrs S. Daglish

Mr M.J. Daniels • Miss E.M. Elms • Mr M. Fox • Mr F. Haydon

Mr G.H. Pinnegar • Mrs G. Poole • Mr K. Richman • Mrs K. Salter

Mr K. Saunders • Mr G. Wirdnam

Doubt exists concerning the original source of some photographs used in this book, many of which have been in the Society Collection for a considerable number of years, and the Swindon Society apologizes for any omissions from the list of acknowledgements given above.